CRITICAL DECISIONS
MADE EASY

Have you ever second-guessed a decision you made in life? Have you ever been paralyzed in fear to such a point that you never move forward in a decision? Have you thought, *If only I had a guide or a mentor who could help me in the process of decision-making*? This book, *Critical Decisions Made Easy,* is a step-by-step guide to help you navigate the essential decision-making process personally and professionally. Rodney Payne uses his personal story of realizing success in the midst of facing challenges to inspire the reader to achieve a personal standard of integrity while making critical decisions. The journey ahead can be challenging, but with the correct steps, your decisions can bring you and your organization incredible success. After reading this book you will truly be able to say, "The *best* is yet to come!"

—Thomas E. Brewer
Author, *God Moments in Time*

Critical Decisions Made Easy is by far the best book I've ever read on decision-making! The way Rodney is able to break down the essential keys to decision-making is palatable, and the framework is simple to follow. After reading this book, I was able to make a critical decision within a fraction of my usual time. Without a doubt, I wholeheartedly recommend *Critical Decisions Made Easy.* My life and the way I make decisions are forever changed.

—Danielle Adams, M.S.Ed.
Owner, Divine Inspirations Professional Services

Rodney Payne is an authentic, compassionate, motivating speaker, leader, coach, and author. His expansive knowledge and expertise across so many professional disciplines are impressive. Through Mr. Payne's courses, publications, and presentations I consistently learn business strategies that help me navigate today's challenges while positioning myself for long-term success. There is a lot to learn and know about effective leadership, and Mr. Payne has the unique ability to tie it all together in a systematic way that allows you to build those skills that position you for success. *Critical Decisions Made Easy* is another example of Mr. Payne's ability to take a difficult subject and make it something everyone can implement effectively with measurable results. Well done!

—Narita Anderson, Ph.D.
Owner, Anderson Estate Planning Solutions

Great communicators, teachers, and coaches take complex principles and make them easy to understand; easy to adapt to one's personal life or organization; and easy to implement for greater results. In his book *Critical Decisions Made Easy* Rodney Payne masterfully does this by allowing individuals, teams, and organizations to clearly identify which decisions are "critical," how to prioritize decisions based on his "cost analysis," determine the optimum solutions, and effectively implement the conclusions. By intentionally following this effective process, the reader will find it becoming a natural lifestyle process in great decision-making.

—Pastor T. L. Bates
OKC Faith Church

Rodney Payne is the real deal—a wise, seasoned, and practical business leader. His new book will change how you think about business and decision-making. *Critical Decisions Made Easy* demonstrates that decision-making and personal growth are integrally related to personal and institutional values. Reading this book will take your life and business to the next level. It is a game-changer!

—Dr. William Valmyr
Speaker, CEO, Transformational Leadership, LLC
Author, *The Vanguard Leader*

John Wooden said, "There is a choice you have to make in everything you do. So keep in mind that in the end, the choice you make makes you." Unfortunately, few of us are ever taught how to make good decisions. In his book *Critical Decisions Made Easy* author Rodney Payne teaches a simple process that anyone can learn to use to find the best answer when faced with tough decisions.

—Chris Robinson
Executive VP Entrepreneurial Solutions Group,
Maxwell Leadership

CRITICAL
DECISIONS
MADE EASY

Dana,

Great leaders are great
decision-makers - Make
great decisions !

Phil 1:6

CRITICAL DECISIONS MADE EASY

RODNEY R. PAYNE

Published by Dust Jacket Press
Critical Decisions Made Easy/Rodney R. Payne

ISBN: 978-1-953285-31-7

Rodney R. Payne
P.O. Box 50485
Midwest City, OK 73140

Cover and interior design by D.E. West, www.zaqdesigns.com
Dust Jacket Press Creative Services

Printed in the United States of America

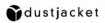

DEDICATION

This book is dedicated to my "home team." That sounds a bit unusual, but my "home team" is my most significant support system and my "why." I have not completed a project to date in which you all have not been present every step of the way. You served as my focus group, encouragement, and accountability partners. I dedicate this book to you, my wife of thirty-two and a half years, Thelma; plus Danielle, Trevel, Jaxen, Teaghan, Tycen, Devin, and Brian—my "home team." I love and appreciate you all!

CONTENTS

ACKNOWLEDGMENTS

Thank you to those who helped this book become a reality. As a person of faith, I find that one of my guiding principles is prayer. Thank you, Arthur, Barbara, and Alivia Campbell, for your prayers for my family and me. A special thank-you to Barbara Campbell for being my writing accountability partner. You are an encourager extraordinaire.

Eban and Tamara Stillwell, thank you for praying this project through! You all prayed, called, emailed, and texted me regularly for progress reports. Your efforts made a difference and kept the project moving along. Thank you!

Finally, I must acknowledge Mr. David Lloyd. Our work together codified the process that has now become the book *Critical Decisions Made Easy.* Your coachability and encouragement provided the evidence and support to know that this is a scalable decision making process. Thank you for being more than a client. Thank you for being a brother and a friend.

INTRODUCTION

One thing I have learned over my twenty-five-year career in corporate America is that many decisions will be made along the way. Decisions serve as the compass for both individuals as well as organizations. When identifying the most impactful leaders I have encountered or observed, one thing is clear: they are all very good at making decisions. While their approaches may differ, every established, successful leader has a particular way of making decisions. As I consider this book's purpose and content, I consider the great need for leaders at every level to have access to a proven decision-making model. While decision-making may be intuitive for some, I believe all decision-makers could benefit from a consistent decision-making process they can depend on.

In the early 1990s I was getting my feet wet in my newfound career in banking and finance. I was in no position to call it a career at all. I was happy to have a job that looked good from the outside—I was in my early twenties starting a job in a bank! I wore a suit and tie every day. I looked very successful as I backed out of the driveway of my recently purchased three-bedroom, two-car-garage, small brick home. If you had asked me at that time, I would tell you that I was living the dream. I had a new family and a new career (job), and it looked as though, to the world at least, I was on my way to realizing the American dream.

REALITY SETS IN . . .

The reality of this dream I was living was that the job (not necessarily a career yet) was very good and the company treated me very well. I learned a lot in a very short time and was upward bound. However, the job didn't pay well enough. Never mind that they hired me with no college degree and minimal experience. What did I expect? Did I expect to be a loan officer from day one? Of course not; I thought that might take a couple of years.

After a series of financial decisions (more like blunders), I desperately needed more money. Yes, the career gave the appearance of success, but we were a sinking ship, taking on water quickly. My wife had a stable job; she is still employed with the same company some thirty years later. Even with her working faithfully and taking on a part-time job, we could not see our way into a better financial situation.

I took on an evening job at a fast-food restaurant, ran a small landscaping company (I mowed a few lawns), and even operated an unlicensed barbershop in my wife's "open concept kitchen/dining room combo" on the weekends to help make ends meet.

IT'S TIME FOR *CRITICAL DECISION* NUMBER ONE . . .

Working at the bank, I was definitely on the fast track to success. I was privileged to train people who made more money than me. That caused a feeling of frustration to set in. The challenge was that the frustration was there, but we often attribute it to the wrong source. I was angry with the bank for hiring someone with a degree and qualified to do a job I was certainly not qualified to do, but I would have hired myself since I was a hard worker.

So here we were at this first critical decision. At the time, I had about three or four jobs, a couple of small children, a very patient wife, and a mortgage. My family was growing but my income was not.

Then I made the critical decision to go back to college, a decision that was critical but also a no-brainer. The bank had a tuition assistance program that paid for two classes per semester, including books. All I had to do was find six hours per week to attend class and whatever time it took to study, be a husband and father, and a *wantrepreneur* (a made-up word I hear Mark Cuban use on the TV show *Shark Tank*). This contrived word described me to a T—I was a want-to-be entrepreneur.

The critical decision to go back to school was in no way easy, but it was very necessary. After all, it took me only five years to earn my A. A. S. (associate in applied science) degree in finance. This decision would ultimately transform my banking career, which would become a career after I committed to going back to college to earn a degree and getting every certification I could in order to move up the corporate ladder.

While I made this decision at a crucial time in my life, I wouldn't have classified it as critical. Rather, I would probably call it a decision born out of desperation and necessity. I suppose it could have been the wrong decision, but I simply did what was intuitive for me—whatever it took to provide for my family.

WHAT IS A *CRITICAL DECISION* ANYWAY?

The British Dictionary via Dictionary.com defines *critical* as "containing careful or analytical evaluations."

Dicitionary.com defines *decision* as "the act or process of deciding; determination, as of a question or doubt, by making a judgment." Leveraging these two resourced definitions, we will use the following as a working definition for a critical decision:

Critical Decision—a decision of the highest priority and significance to an individual or organization's next steps in the growth process.

Based on our working definition, a definitive line is drawn between decisions. Not all decisions are critical. You will make many decisions as a leader, but not all of them will be critical. Therefore, leaders must easily differentiate between critical decisions and all other decisions. The simplest way to determine the level of a decision is to consider the expected consequence of the decision. There are many considerations in determining the consequences of a decision. In this book we will look at a three-step process that I have crafted to help me make decisions. I have used this model when making decisions for myself and my clients. Implementing these steps is very effective in every type of decision. I have used this process to make critical decisions impacting individuals' lives. The critical decision process has also been an effective model for making decisions in the professional or corporate space. I have also used this same process and found success in the faith-based community. Just imagine yourself with a tool that works in every area of your life!

Critical Decisions Made Easy will take you through a detailed process of *qualification, quantification,* and *execution,* ultimately giving you a tool you can master and use confidently. Every decision becomes additive evidence to help you with your next critical decision.

CHAPTER ONE

Qualification

As the week begins, every leader faces a litany of decisions that must be made by some predetermined deadline. Just picture yourself sitting behind your desk with your neatly organized stacks of files and papers strategically placed in the order you plan to address them. While gazing at this overwhelming stack of files, you log on to your computer while retrieving a freshly brewed cup of your favorite coffee.

Just as you click on your email icon on your computer, your inbox begins to fill as if someone is playing a cruel joke on you. In addition to your desk being covered and your inbox being filled, you have others who have decided they need you critically, so they have decided to text you.

At the risk of causing you to close this book, I will forego the red indicator light on your voicemail and the notification that your mandatory staff meeting is about to start in five minutes. Did I mention the text from your spouse reminding you of your family commitments that await you as soon as you get off for the day? Oh, yeah—and don't forget the new workout regimen you committed to (only because your doctor said you needed to do something).

Honestly, I could continue adding to this list for several more pages, but you get the picture. So many things are vying for your attention that it can almost become mind-blowing. So many obligations and responsibilities pull you simultaneously in different directions. How do you make sense of it? This chapter will look at step one of the critical decision-making process.

Qualification. What exactly is qualification? According to Dictionary.com, qualification is a condition that modifies or limits restriction. As you consider your decision-making process, there must be some conditions established that help limit or restrict things that can gain priority access to one of your most valuable assets—time. If given the opportunity, everyone and everything would like always to be in the priority position of your life. So many people need a minute from you—they can't live without your input. Everything is a squeaky wheel, demanding your attention immediately.

The challenge for many leaders is self-imposed guilt. We place unwarranted guilt upon ourselves because of expectations placed on us by others. Before we can go more deeply into qualification, we must establish some ground rules.

GROUND RULES

1. Not every decision is **critical**.

2. *Critical* for others **does not** necessarily mean *critical* for you.

3. You must be **consistent** in identifying critical decisions.

4. You need a **system** for handling critical decisions.

Now that we have established some ground rules, we need to "qualify for qualification." To qualify, we must first *identify* the decision at hand. Identifying the decision is a relatively simple process. If it's before you are awaiting a response, then it is a decision. But just being recognized as a decision is not enough. You see, an already-established system can make many decisions. For example, if we have standard procedures in place, we can apply the rules of the standard procedure without giving time or energy to the decision. So yes, a decision must be made, but it is not critical.

So how do we differentiate between decisions and critical decisions? We *qualify* them. How do we qualify decisions? Going back to our definition earlier in this chapter, we must set some conditions by establishing a process for qualification. Our process of qualification is a three-step process:

1. Assess
2. Articulate
3. Align

STEP 1: ASSESS

Assessment in the qualification stage determines which decision bucket a decision should land in. Is the decision critical or uncritical? Remember: our goal is to establish processes whereby some decisions can be moved from critical to uncritical. The process of assessing the decision begins with the end in mind. Decision assessment happens at a very high level.

Is the decision yours to make? Leaders generally work with teams. In working with teams, many decisions that should have been made long before they arrived at you can end up on your desk. To properly assess a decision, you must make sure it is your decision to make. If the decision is not yours, it cannot be considered critical. Even if your agreement is needed to finalize the decision, it should not be given critical status.

Once you determine that the decision is yours, you need to assess who will be impacted by the decision. The goal is to give the necessary attention to critical decisions, and having a narrow view will limit your ability to assess the decision properly. Considering whom the decision will impact during the assessment will save you time and give you invaluable data you will use in the second step of the decision-making process.

> Leaders who are empowered and trusted know they are valued.

The final step in assessing the decision is to answer the question "Can I delegate this decision/process to one of my team members to effectively handle it?" Earlier in this chapter I advised you to consider if the decision was yours to make. The delegation process identifies that the decision is yours to make, but it is not so critical that *you* must make it. That is when delegation comes in. You can extend your authority to a qualified team member, empowering him or her to decide on your behalf. This process comes with benefits. The first benefit is that empowered leaders become more of an asset to your team. When you empower a leader, it demonstrates your trust and your confidence in him or her. Leaders who are empowered and trusted know they are valued.

Everyone wants to be appreciated. When a leader knows that he or she is appreciated, the leader's perspective changes as he or she moves from just doing his or her part to genuinely having some skin in the game. You want leaders who become stakeholders and consider themselves integral parts of your team.

Another benefit is that empowered leaders will lighten your load. The more you delegate to qualified leaders on your team, the more you extend yourself as a leader. The present investment you make in your decision-making process will pay big dividends in the future. As a word of caution, however, leaders unwilling to invest in leadership development and empowerment on the front end often pay the price of burnout on the back end.

STEP 2: ARTICULATE

Once we have placed the decision under the assessment microscope, we move to the second step in the qualification part of the decision-making process: *articulation.* Articulation is expressing an idea or a feeling fluently or coherently. Once you have assessed the decision, you must be able to capture it thoroughly and express it in a way that makes sense.

The leader must pay attention to a few steps in the articulation process. The decision must be organized, revised, and communicated accordingly.

Organizing a decision begins with honestly considering your assessment of the decision. Although it's not always convenient to be transparent and honest with yourself in decision-making, it's 100-percent necessary. Organizing goes beyond just merely putting something in sequential order. Organizing a decision looks at the past, present, and future impact of the decision.

The past consideration of a decision looks at the "How did we get here?" of the decision. Was there something that happened to cause this decision that could have been avoided through more diligence in consideration of a previous decision? Considering "How did we get here?" can often prevent you from being in this place again. When we take the time to look back, it allows us to create and implement systems to handle these types of decisions in the future. Ultimately it helps us to become more efficient in our processes because we took the time to look back, which helps us to learn from the past.

We must also take time to look at the present circumstances surrounding the decision at hand. While looking back at the past helps us to learn from history, looking at the present allows us to get the best out of the situation now and to prepare for the future.

Looking at the present can be a very emotional process. Why is this? Because the present includes all the confusion and chaos captured in the everyday life of a leader. Several individual fires may burn simultaneously, and you have only so much water as a leader. The fires are coming from every direction—personnel, process, vendor, contractor, and family—all at the same time. How we address and respond to decisions in a very emotional "present" is critical.

We must be cautious not to make emotional decisions without proper consideration. Here is where proper identification of a critical decision is—you guessed it—*critical.* Is it necessary for it to be addressed right now? If not, immediately place the decision in the proper storage place until you are not so emotional. That will allow you to revisit the decision with the appropriate mindset and proper considerations.

Unfortunately, some present conditions will *not* be ignored and will not cooperate with being placed on the back burner. What do you do when you're forced to deal with the "right now" of a decision? First, you must engage your experience and rely on the past. What similar situations have you faced that would be helpful in this situation? It's often said that experience is the best teacher. While I agree that experience can be a great teacher, I would like to challenge you to get more out of your experience, the key to which is to leverage more than just the facts of the experience. The facts are the *what, when, where, why,* and *who* of the decision. These elements are indeed critical. In addition, however, I would like you to consider the *process you leveraged* when considering all these elements to arrive ultimately at your decision. The process is transferable. Remember: when I have a process, I can apply it to any situation and arrive at a reasonable conclusion that's fact based.

Finally is the future consideration of qualification. How does the qualification of this decision impact my future? Improper qualification of a decision puts the decision at risk of becoming a decision that produces a negative residual result. The goal in considering the future is to position yourself for success in the future. Viewing the end in the present can set a precedence for developing a new, more effective process.

It's often said that the past shapes the future. The main goal at this stage is to intentionally consider the future impact of how we qualify decisions. As a leader's responsibilities increase, qualification becomes more critical. Your leadership capacity is greatly diminished when you cannot distinguish between critical and uncritical decisions. The main reason for this decreased capacity is that your efficacy is negatively impacted when you fail to anticipate and plan for the time component of giving your attention to uncritical items.

A leader's energy has a ceiling. Every day has a time limit. Only 24 hours, 1,440 minutes, and 86,400 seconds are allotted daily. This is the same for everyone, with no exceptions. Within that time you are expected to live, eat, sleep, have a personal life, and be a leader. More times than not, leaders have too much on their to-do lists. They are always looking for "extra" time to squeeze one more thing into their day. Therefore, qualification is extremely critical for making the best decisions.

For qualification to be a completed process, remember that you must assess. The assessment phase serves as the foundational stage of qualification. Is the decision critical? Is the decision yours to make? And finally, can you delegate this decision to a qualified team member?

Remember that you can delegate only a decision that you can articulate successfully. Articulation requires you to express an idea or a feeling fluently or coherently. There truly is an art to getting your thoughts out of your head! This takes intentionality and practice. It will take some time and effort, but you can do it. I recommend that leaders write their thoughts on a whiteboard or a piece of paper and use an app to record them. Once you capture them, you must revisit them to digest and organize your thoughts. Following this process will help you articulate your ideas to others.

Now that you have prepared the way to complete step one in the critical decision-making process, you're ready to wrap a nice little bow around your decisions. You must complete the assessment and articulation phases to move to this final step.

STEP 3: ALIGN

The final step of the qualification process is *alignment*. According to Dictionary.com, *align* is "to arrange in a straight line; adjust according to a line. To bring into cooperation or agreement with." As you begin unpacking the alignment phase, some key factors must be considered. Your decision-making alignment is only as good as the key indicators governing your alignment. These indicators will serve as the "straight line" that will guide qualification for all of your decisions. These key indications will guide you through the entire critical decision-making process.

So what are these indicators, and how do you leverage them in the decision-making process? The key indicators in the alignment process are your guiding principles, associations, and *why*.

Let's start with your guiding principles, which are based on your personal beliefs and values. Your belief system and personal beliefs establish the boundaries and guidelines for how you lead every area of your life.

I am a person of faith. As a result, my faith serves as the plumb line for every decision I make, whether good or bad, right or wrong. My faith sets a fixed "straight line" to guide my decisions. Without a static straight line beyond your thoughts and feelings to guide your decisions, you are left only with the momentary and unstable tools of your thoughts, feelings, and emotions to guide your decisions, which is a dangerous and volatile way to make decisions.

So how do you activate your belief system in critical decision-making? You must operate with discipline by accepting your external standard as the only measuring stick for your decisions. You should never make decisions that disagree with your belief system. Why is this so important? Since there are so many factors that can influence your decisions, having a consistent belief system will assist in bringing your decisions to their full potential for helping shape your desired brand.

Your desired brand is realized only when you make consistent decisions, which require a continuous straight line to be measured. Take some time to identify your belief system. Once you have done that, you must invest in fully adopting your belief system. Your belief system should not be a system you would "like to" follow; rather, it must be the way you truly make decisions. A critical reminder is that your belief system must be consistent in every area. As a decision-maker, you want to use the same standard in every area of your life. A belief system is not situational; it is a personal conviction best used when applied to every area of your life.

Now let's talk values. Values are the components of your belief system that ultimately keep you in line with your belief systems, such as honesty, integrity, dependability, and commitment. Values are the outwardly visible traits that express the internal compass of your guiding belief system.

Values are important because many external thoughts, ideas, and motivations seek to weigh in on your decision-making process. If you don't truly establish your values, you cannot successfully identify or achieve the desired outcome. For instance, when you make money your goal without establishing values, you position yourself in an anything-goes position. While at the surface this may not seem like a big deal, the absence of values introduces risk factors that could ultimately derail your success.

Values help to keep you in a straight line of achieving your goals. The challenge with values, even when they're your own values, is that they're only sometimes easy, convenient, or comfortable to adhere to. When carefully thought out, values always have your best interests in mind and bring out the best in you. However, they don't often allow for shortcuts.

> Values help to keep you in a straight line of achieving your goals.

Values will lead you along the high road. John Maxwell has often shared, "Anything worthwhile is uphill all the way." Strong values will keep you climbing the hill on the front end, but by keeping good values in place, many destructive risks will be avoided entirely.

In making critical decisions, many decisions will be "automatically" disqualified. This is a vital qualification step in the critical decision-making process. You

> If you have "flexible" values, you have no values at all.

are ahead whenever you can have standards that reduce the time required in the decision-making process.

The "automatic" component is activated when you're looking to make a decision and, presented with a decision, you automatically see that it falls outside of your values or your belief system; you don't invest any more time in this decision because it's immediately or "automatically" disqualified.

The key here is to avoid looking for workarounds related to your values and belief system. Your values must be a hard line. If they're important enough to you to be established as one or more of your values, then they're important enough to be adhered to. If you have "flexible" values, you have no values at all.

Alignment serves the leader's decision-making process much as a front-end alignment on a car serves the driver of the vehicle. When you take your vehicle in for service at your local automobile repair shop to purchase tires, the service person usually recommends getting all new tires and a wheel alignment, for which there are many benefits. The alignment makes it easier for the driver to keep the vehicle going straight. Additionally, the tires wear more evenly and last longer.

When making critical decisions, you want to make sure they help keep you on a straight line so you can get from where you are to where you want to go. Values are essential to keeping you "in line" and can make the critical decision process easy.

QUALIFICATION: A QUICK LOOK BACK

There are three steps in the qualification process: *assessment, articulation,* and *alignment. Assessment* qualifies the decision as critical or not. It determines if the decision is even yours to make. *Articulation* packages the decision in a communicable form. Qualification is nearly impossible if you can't get the decision out of your head. Finally, *alignment* is the qualifier that helps you determine if a decision aligns with your motivating factors and guiding principles. When you take the time to establish and develop your guiding principles, you take the guesswork out of making decisions. You can "automatically" disqualify decisions that do not align with your guiding principles.

ACTION STEPS

Now you can begin to make your decision-making process easy by implementing the qualification step in the decision-making process.

STEP 1 - DECLUTTER

Decluttering is not much fun, but it's essential! You might not like this part of the process very much, but you'll thank me later.

In the decluttering phase, you must take a complete inventory of your life. That's right—I said your life. Once you catch your breath, keep reading. It's time to go through everything that comes across your desk from every area of your life. Once you get them separated into macro-categories, such as work, personal life, family life, personal brand, church, and so on, you can start to figure out what to do.

If you haven't touched it, you can probably discard it. This may be painful, but seriously—let it go!

STEP 2 - DELEGATE

Once you declutter, you'll find you still have way too much on your desk that's optional, and it requires your hands-on attention to move forward. You can begin delegating these piles to others for effective execution. When I say *delegate,* I do not mean *abandon.* Delegation is designating someone to represent you in a given capacity or task. To delegate effectively, you must commit to a few things. Delegation requires equipping, authority, and accountability.

You can give someone the responsibility of making decisions on your behalf only if you have properly equipped him or her for the task. While the ultimate goal of this book is to help you make critical decisions, I'll spend a little more time on this step. Equipping can happen through various processes, but it should always include a good relationship, a clear understanding of your guiding principles, and enough information to make the decision.

Authority is much like a power of attorney, which grants someone the authority to act on your behalf. Just by definition, we can ascertain that this is a huge deal. To give someone power of attorney to make decisions on your behalf should be a decision you make only with a very thoughtful and deliberate process. Once you go through the qualifying process of those you're willing to grant authority to for acting on your behalf, you must authorize them. As a consideration, delegation that requires you to review every decision before it is made is not delegation; it is nothing more than having someone do the leg work to prepare you to make the decision yourself. While this may be beneficial, it will not help you in delegating those decisions within your organization that could be handled by someone else. The goal of freeing up your time to focus on those micro-buckets still left on your desk.

Finally, anyone you trust enough to give the power of attorney to in order to make decisions on your behalf must be held accountable. Delegation is not a "set it and forget it" process. Just because you've given someone the authority to make such decisions doesn't mean the person is not answerable for the decisions he or she makes. Ultimately, you should have a system in place, a regular meeting time or reporting structure for those to whom you've delegated some of your decision-making. This doesn't mean you need to review every single decision but rather inspect the decision-making process and outcomes of those decisions. Whether or not the person is making the same decision you would make is not really what you're reviewing. You're inspecting what the motivating factors are behind the decisions this person makes. Are these factors adherent to your guiding principles? Are they getting the desired results? When you take the time to inspect what you expect, you gain the benefit of achieving your desired outcomes and growing your leaders/decision-makers simultaneously.

The delegation will ultimately free up time on your calendar—but you'll have to pay on the front end before you can reap the harvest of more time on the back end.

STEP 3 - DECIDE

Finally, you must decide. Remember: we are only in step one of the critical decision-making process. So what you need to do at this stage is to determine if this decision qualifies as a critical decision. By now you have spent much time getting things in order, and the decision-making process might seem a bit overwhelming. Let me remind you that the first time is the most challenging. You're building a system that will impact all future decisions. This system will not just affect your decisions but will also allow you to have automated steps in your qualification process. These steps not only facilitate your decision-making but also add consistency to it. Consistency helps you to validate your "gut feeling." Many of us make certain decisions every day because they just feel right. Adding a qualification process to your decision-making helps you decide how much time and attention you'll give to any specific decision. Doing this on the front end is a game-changer. Just think about the time when you spent way too many hours counting on a decision that ended up being irrelevant. What if you had a system that could have saved you all that wasted time?

In a nutshell, that's just what the qualification process does. It helps you determine if this decision is critical. If it is, you'll learn in the coming chapters how to decide. If the decision is not critical, however, you'll relocate it to the appropriate place.

Remember: qualification requires *assessment, articulation,* and *alignment.* Once you assess, you then articulate, align, discard, delegate—or decide.

CHAPTER TWO

Quantification

As we continue the critical decision-making journey, our next step is *quantification.* Quantification is the process of determining the costs of the decision. Every decision comes with unavoidable costs. The goal of the quantification stage is to determine if the costs of any decision are significant enough to qualify it as critical.

The key to the entire decision-making process is to avoid entertaining uncritical decisions. Remember: the decision-maker's time capital is minimal and usually well expended. As a result, we want to help the decision-maker make the most of his or her time.

While we know every decision comes with inherent costs, how does the leader quantify these costs? In this section we will take you through a particular process of counting the costs. The ability to accurately count the costs will distance an effective leader from others. While this ability is innate to some leaders, most decision-makers could greatly benefit from a tried-and-true, reproducible process of quantification.

> The ability to accurately count the costs will distance an effective leader from others.

Now buckle up as we go through developing a system of quantification, in which you'll need to assess the value of your costs, evaluate your costs, and finally respond to your results. This complex system may be challenging to establish, but once established, it will significantly reduce the stress and wasted time of the decision-maker.

ASSESS THE VALUE OF YOUR COSTS

Have you ever considered the actual costs of your decision-making process before making a decision? Just think—posthumously counting costs is easy but provides little benefit to decision-making unless you leverage this intel in making future decisions. The problem for most leaders is that their queue is always full of the "right-now" decisions.

Leaders often figure out how to capitalize on super-productive moments to get caught up or get everything done on their lists. The problem with this method is that there is no simple process. As a result, the leader needs more control when these super-productive moments appear. I love it when I get into super-productive moments, days, or weeks! I can sometimes push out three or four days of work in one day! I love it! I like to call it "blowing and going"—I'm "blowing" through my work and "going" to the next item on my list!

Unfortunately, those super-productive moments don't come as often as I would like. That's why leaders need systems to help with productivity and efficiency. Believe it or not, we can develop a reproducible process for quantifying our decisions.

Let me first identify the things we'll consider in our quantification process. As leaders who are called upon to make many critical decisions, we cannot afford to miss them. Consequently, we need to consider six issues in the quantification process.

> Leaders need systems to help with productivity and efficiency.

CONSIDERATION ONE: TIME

Time. What role does time play in the decision-making process? Why is time so important? You guessed it—we don't have enough of it, or at least that's the excuse we like to use. The reality of time is that it's very definable. Time is allotted to all leaders in the same quantity, with no exceptions. We are all restricted to the same 1,440 minutes per day, 24 hours per day, and 365 days per year, except for leap year, which has 366 days. That's it! No one gets any more time.

Now that we're on a level playing field, we should be able to agree on one fact: *we do not have enough time to waste time.* Time impacts the decision-making process in three ways. First, we must set aside time to make the decision. Second, decision-making must be a priority. And third, we must deal with the residual time impact of the decision.

So let's dig into finding the time even to decide. With all the demands on a leader's time, the easiest way to make decisions is to give your attention to the "squeaky wheel." Whatever is making the most noise must deserve your immediate attention, right? Wrong! Noise does not necessarily make the decision a priority; noise only guarantees that whatever the problem is has become a nuisance. The most effective way to find time to make decisions is to define a specific time for making decisions. When you set the time, you can also select other conditions favorable to good decision-making. As we discussed earlier, effective systems are critical to making critical decisions. When you set the time, you can also set the environment, establish your best decision-making state of mind, and even limit or eliminate external distractions.

When choosing your time, make sure you choose a time when you are most mentally alert and focused. I'm an early riser (yes, I'm one of those morning people). In the morning my energy and focus are better, my mindset is better, and my efficiency and productivity are even better. Knowing yourself is part of making decisions and getting the most out of your time. I have learned that if I end my day by planning the next day with the most critical thought items as a priority, I am better and get them done more effectively. There's also a bonus to my making decisions early in the day. I work more quickly and efficiently in my most productive time. For example, it may take me two hours of contemplation to decide after 2:00 p.m. The same decision and considerations can be made in less than half of the time if I address them before 8:00 a.m. That sounds unbelievable, but I'm definitely more fruitful when fresh and focused. When making critical decisions, identify your most productive time when you're least likely to be distracted, and you'll see your frustrations significantly reduced.

Decision-making must be viewed as a priority. Putting off a critical decision to an undetermined time is not an option. As a leader, you must keep your priorities in order. The quantification process requires proper assignment of priority. As we dealt with earlier, qualification should have gotten any uncritical decisions off your plate. Critical decisions must be on the top of your list in the limited resource of time you have daily.

I have a few tips to help you in the prioritization process. One of the very vital components of making critical decisions is research. While leaders need the details to make the correct decision, many leaders do not have the time to research to get the much-needed facts. As we've already established, high-capacity leaders usually have more to do than they can get done on any given day. Leaders cannot afford to shortcut the critical decision-making process by leaving out the details—or can they? No shortcut will cover the risk associated with leaving out the details. Still, the leader can, in some cases, delegate the research component to a team member. Delegating a time-consuming task such as research can help a leader reclaim some of the valuable time lost in the grinding process of leadership.

Delegation can be a great tool, but it must be used cautiously. Some critical decisions are highly confidential. So whenever considering delegation as a time-redeeming tool, always consider the sensitivity, confidentiality, and impact

> Our efficiency comes through fire *prevention*, not fire *fighting*.

of others having access to the "research."

In addition to delegation, awareness and planning are also keys to the prioritization process. John Maxwell's law of awareness states, "You must know yourself to grow yourself." You knowing yourself will always be your most significant asset. Knowing yourself is key to maximizing productivity and making the most beneficial decision. You know what you can handle and what you cannot. Many people will try redirecting your focus or behavior to what *they* think is best for you. However, you know some things about yourself that others do not know. You know what you can delegate and what you cannot. You know what you can, in essence, let go of and what you cannot. Awareness helps you save time by maximizing your strengths and mitigating your weaknesses.

Prioritization is easier said than done. There may be better places to give your attention first than the squeaky wheel. Prioritization is ranking, usually in the order of priority or significance. When prioritizing decisions, it's beneficial to have a process in place. I know we keep coming back to the process to avoid the time-consuming fire drill decision-making process. We don't want to spend time fighting fires. Our efficiency comes through fire *preven-tion,* not fire*fighting.* While not every fire can be avoided, many can be avoided simply by having a process. Prioritiza-tion helps us keep our various decision types in the proper buckets and lets us get to the most critical and time-sensi-tive decisions first.

As stated earlier, time is a limited resource. The most effective leaders are strong decision-makers. Making quan-tification of your time a priority will help you get the most out of your leadership journey.

CONSIDERATION TWO: MONEY

Money is the reason we all lead, right? Wrong! Money is simply a tool necessary to operate a business. Many people in leadership roles are often motivated by money. Money is not the best motivator. When it's the primary motivation, it can quickly become the source of great pain and turmoil for the leader. Money can be either positive or negative. The key is how the leader chooses to use it. A responsible leader must always consider the financial costs associated with a decision. While the financial impact should be con-sidered, there must be other considerations. The leader must, of course, consider the immediate financial impact of the decision, the *people* impact, and ultimately the future impact of the decision. He or she should consider three primary areas regarding money when quantifying the cost of a decision.

First, *Can we financially afford this decision?* Believe it or not, this is not a question best answered by looking at the bank account balance. Answering the question "Can we afford the decision?" is a decision best made by—you guessed it—planning and process. If you must look at your bank balance before deciding, the quick answer is that you *cannot* afford it.

This question leads to another one: *How can I know if I can afford the decision without checking my bank balance?* As a leader tasked with making affordable decisions, you can plan for them. That's right—you can build a financial system and discipline to prepare for critical decisions. Many times decisions seem to be essential decisions that must be made now, and we need money now! While that may be the immediate symptom, in many cases it could have been avoided with a proper plan.

I will avoid making this a financial management and budgeting segment of this book. I'll simply give you tips for developing a financial system to help you in your critical decision-quantification process.

When a leader does not start with a plan, he or she often proves the truth of the old adage "When we fail to plan, we plan to fail." As we discussed in the introduction of this book, every leader must have guiding principles. Financial guiding principles require thought and a particular strategy. For example, if we plan to be a cash-only brand that will not operate from a place of debt, we must have a cash flow system to support that principle. In this example, we know we plan to work on a cash basis. As a result, we build cash reserves, never borrow money, and clearly define our spending criteria. Not to oversimplify the process, but by making decisions beforehand we develop healthy habits that support our guiding principles and position us to make critical decisions accordingly. Suppose we must decide at any point in the critical decision-making process to proceed or to stop on a particular decision. In that case, we can refer to our guiding principles, and our predetermined process can help in making critical decisions.

Now let's talk about the *people* impact of money. As stated earlier, the acquisition of talented team members can be an expensive proposition. There is the expense of location, recruitment, hiring, onboarding, and training of new team members before you ever begin to see a return on your investment. Additionally, the people of your business are your business.

So the financial impact can make or break a business when making people decisions. Hiring the right team members certainly helps to mitigate the people expense. However, hiring is only the first step in the process. Once you add the new team member, the training, relationship building, empowerment, and accountability come into play. Whether a professional hiring transaction or a personal relationship, the financial impact can be significant when we miss it in the people process. Whether we befriend the wrong person, hire the wrong person, or even lose the wrong person, the financial impact can be long-lasting.

The most important thing in the people process is to remember that *you're dealing with people!* People can be an asset or your most significant expense. Consider people more than assets, resources, or team members. Consider *valuing* people. That's right—valuing people will take you a long way to properly managing your people expenses. One of the most impactful observations from my mentor John C. Maxwell is the well-known saying "People don't care how much you know until they know how much you care." People desire to be valued. People want to know they matter to you more than simply what they can do for you.

> People want to know they matter to you more than simply what they can do for you.

As leaders with the tremendous responsibility of making critical decisions, we can sometimes forget to value people. When that happens, we put ourselves at risk of incurring significant expenses. We lose valuable team members because we failed to value them. We can become so mission-minded that we forget it's the people who deliver the mission. Even in making a critical personal decision, when we undervalue or take advantage of people, it can cost us down the road.

> The art of quantifying the future cost of a present decision separates a good leader from a great leader.

As a leader, you must make the critical decision to invest in solid and healthy relationships with those around you to avoid paying the high costs of having the wrong people around you. Establish guiding principles that foster a people-before-profit mentality, and you'll position yourself to extend yourself to maximum capacity by having the best people around you. When you take the time to build this people process, you'll reduce your people expenses and increase your productivity and profitability and make better decisions because of the team around you.

Properly quantifying your people costs will make your critical decision-making process one of your strong points. Good people make *you* better. Be willing to pay a few more dollars on the front end to save more on the back end.

Finally, let's talk about the future impact of the decision. The art of quantifying the future cost of a present decision separates a good leader from a great leader. Many people attribute the skill of speculation, intuition, or just plain good old instincts to the success of many leaders. While I believe some leaders are gifted, as stated above, I also believe you can develop a system for quantifying the future impact of a critical decision.

The system does not have to be complicated, but the system needs to be consistent. What data will you consider in determining the future impact? While it's not an exhaustive list, if you consider your experience, consider the facts of your present situation, and apply your guiding principles, you'll position yourself to make a better decision for your future.

CONSIDERATION THREE: MORAL STANDARDS

Considering your moral standards in the quantification process ensures that you never ignore your guiding principles in your critical decision-making process. You'll find that the more guardrails you have to keep you on track, the fewer critical decisions you'll face. The key to moral standards is that they are personal. *You* get to decide. *You* get to determine what determines right or wrong for you as a leader.

Leaders often desire to have a specific set of moral standards but lack conviction. Being desirous of good moral standards is commendable, but it's not enough to establish good moral standards for leaders. The admiration of other successful leaders could influence the desire. Again, admiration is a good start; it may even lead to desire, but neither is it enough. The leader must be convicted to commit himself or herself to these good moral standards. When there is no personal commitment or conviction to good morals, they become optional in your critical decision-making process.

So how does the leader commit to good moral standards? You guessed it—refer to your guiding principles! In the quantification process, you want a predetermined guide to keeping you focused during the critical decision-making process. When guiding principles are already in place, it becomes a simple assessment rather than a critical decision. As a leader, you must be willing to adhere to your guiding principles. Does it fit—yes or no? There is no "maybe" when it comes to moral standards. Either it complies with the moral standards you've established or it does not.

The moral standards clause is intentionally set in place to protect you from the emotion of attractive opportunities. Moral standards protect you from the shiny get-rich-quick options that could cloud your otherwise-sound judgment. While the opportunity may pan out exactly the way it was presented and no one would be the wiser, a negative residual impact could stain your brand for years to come. As a leader, you must always protect your brand.

You could be presented with an attractive immoral opportunity as a test of character and integrity. You could be unknowingly backing yourself into a corner. It all looks good on the front end. It even appears to work in your favor, but down the road that same opportunity could obligate you to engage in more immoral activity. What you saw as a quick buck or an easy profit becomes a daunting debt. When you decided to engage in the initial opportunity, you told yourself it would be just this one time. While you were well-intentioned, it was so easy, you had no problems—or at least that's how it appeared. Your lack of good moral standards has you backtracking in trying to preserve your good reputation.

Protect your brand. Be thoughtful, intentional, and consistent when determining your moral standards. Move beyond desiring to have a good moral standard to being *committed* to having good moral standards. Take the time to believe in what you want to stand for, and then stand on it! The term *moral failure* has become far too common among high-capacity leaders. You define your moral standards by choosing what will serve as your guiding principles. Being a person of faith, I find that my faith serves as the compass for my "true north." I am neither good enough nor consistent enough to serve as my own compass. As a result, I have adopted the principles of my faith to be my moral standard. Because of this decision, others do not determine my moral success or failure—my faith does. You must have a set of moral standards consistent with being consistently effective in your decision-making process.

Decide to adhere to good moral standards before facing a critical decision, and you've taken a big step in making your critical decision easy.

CONSIDERATION FOUR: HARD VERSUS SOFT COSTS

As we continue assessing costs, let me transition to hard costs versus soft costs. *Hard costs* and *soft costs* are terms generally used in the construction industry. Separating hard costs from soft costs is critical for meeting budgets. Hard costs are easy to determine as they are usually associated with the physical construction items required to complete the project, such as raw materials, labor, equipment, and so on. While just as significant, soft costs may not be as easy to identify. Soft costs include processes such as administration, planning, and general overhead.

Critical decision-making has similar considerations. Earlier we went into detail regarding the monetary impact of the decision-making process. Our emphasis there was on the monetary costs associated with deciding. We want to make sure we were making sound financial decisions. As we consider hard and soft costs, we'll seek to gain in-depth insights to make better-informed decisions.

So let's examine the hard costs of making a critical decision. As in the construction industry, the leader must consider the hard costs. The leader must quantify the hard physical costs of dollars and cents. What do we need to purchase? How many people do we need to carry out this decision effectively? Are there any discounts available for a more significant purchase? Can we combine more than one project's needs within this purchase order?

Many times a leader will offer a discount to earn business. This can be great; who doesn't like a good deal? The leader doesn't want a discount, however, when it comes to a financial loss to the company. Leaders must always be aware of the hard costs.

I'm a fan of the hit television show *Shark Tank* on ABC, which features real-life millionaires and billionaires looking to invest in an entrepreneur's dream. One of the most common mistakes novice entrepreneurs make on the show is that they cannot articulate their numbers effectively. They don't know the hard costs associated with making their products. When you don't know what a decision costs you, the chance of making a good decision is very low.

However, hard costs are only a part of the process. Leaders must also know how to identify and quantify soft costs. What are the soft costs of the critical decision-making process? They include what it takes to get your product or service to market. They include the inconvenience of making incorrect decisions. They also include the overhead of your business.

Soft costs can be compared to an individual who purchases a car and considers only the monthly car payment amount. The new-car owner is excited about his or her shiny new car and is eager to drive off the lot. Some new-car owners will consider the "other" costs—the soft costs. Has the excited new car owner considered the cost of insurance, fuel, upkeep, and ongoing maintenance, or has the payment alone already maxed out the person's budget? Failure to consider the soft costs could put the new-car owner in a position to lose his or her new toy.

As a leader who faces critical decisions regularly, you'll find that counting the costs will separate you from other decision-makers. You're making informed decisions when you count all the costs associated with the decision. When you know your numbers, you can make confident decisions and avoid many negative consequences. By this point it should go without saying, but I'll say it anyway—it's vitally important to develop a system or a process for determining hard and soft costs. Whether it's for your team at work or to purchase that new car for your family, *know your numbers.* Count the costs.

CONSIDERATION FIVE:
THE IF-THEN EQUATION

The "if-then" equation is a leader's deliberate intention to consider various possible outcomes because of a critical decision. This process can seem a bit cumbersome, but it's necessary. Merriam-Webster Dictionary defines *if-then* as an adjective describing a conditional or hypothetical situation. As we merge this term into the decision-making process, the responsible leader must do his or her best to account for various hypothetical conditions. This is necessary because things do not always go according to plan. Often the leader has a well-thought-out strategy; one thing changes and impacts the desired outcome.

Just consider the number of unintended consequences you may have experienced on your leadership journey. As a leader, you have completed all the necessary research, engaged all the right players, and even used conservative projections, only to find that one of your competitors has beat you to market with a similar solution. When you developed your product or service, it was cutting edge, and none of your competitors even came close to offering a product that could deliver what you could provide.

Consequently, you didn't have an if-then strategy to compensate for this unforeseen competition. That, my friend, is a clear example of the power of the if-then equation. Had we considered the possibility of competition, we could have possibly made some adjustments or considerations to help mitigate the risk associated with the competition.

Leroy Eims said, "A leader is one who sees more than others see, who sees farther than others see, and who sees before others see." The if-then equation is a direct result of the leader's ability to see more and to see before others do.

The if-then equation can be reduced to a three-step process. Again, we're still hanging on to our processes and systems. We build them once, implement them, adhere to them, and inspect them. Our systems put guardrails in place to help us in critical decision-making.

So step one in the if-then equation is to identify all up-front costs. Up-front costs are inclusive of all hard and soft costs. Up-front costs also include the strategy associated with delivering the solution. In the previous section of this book we spoke about knowing your numbers. Not only does the if-then equation require the leader to know his or her numbers, but the leader must also know his or her desired outcome. In brief, the leader must know what he or she wants and how much it will cost.

Step two is to identify changes. The leader must pre-identify any anticipat-

> Our systems put guardrails in place to help us in critical decision-making.

> Instincts are good, but preparation is better!

ed changes in the process. While there is no way to know what will happen, the leader can use historical data, industry news, and market awareness to prepare for potential changes. For instance, if the global economy changes during your process, how could that impact your hard and soft costs? The leader's ability to be aware of trends and ahead of the curve equips him or her to make better decisions. Many leaders have great instincts. Instincts are good, but preparation is better! The prepared leader will always employ the if-then equation to help minimize the risk associated with the critical decision-making process.

Step three is to identify challenges. Every decision comes with potential challenges. Challenges can stop a deal in its tracks. In the if-then equation of the quantification process, leaders run multiple hypothetical models to uncover potential challenges. Again, there is no way for the leader to identify all possible challenges. Still, prepared leaders intentionally make better decisions because they look for any obstacle that could hinder their path to success. When the leader identifies challenges, that's a good thing; however, if he or she fails to recognize the "then" when the "if" happens, the challenge is identified but not avoided. Once the leader determines the challenge, what next? What's the best possible solution for the challenge the leader is facing?

When the leader takes the time to make the if-then equation a regular part of his or her quantification process, then efficacy, productivity, and good decision-making become the order of the day. When the leader already knows what he or she will do "if" this happens, "then" the leader is positioned for success. Always know your if-then equation for every decision.

CONSIDERATION SIX: RESIDUAL COSTS/BENEFITS

Earlier we discussed hard versus soft costs. You were encouraged to count all costs associated with a critical decision. The term *residual* references the remainder or leftover residue from a previous action. So as we consider residual costs associated with a critical decision, we're not looking at simply a one-time future consequence of a decision but rather the residual or ongoing costs. Ongoing costs can be a little tricky to catch. Why? Because they're often more challenging to identify.

Here are a few key questions when uncovering and quantifying residual costs: *What areas will be affected by this decision? How do I replace the function of this decision?*

How long will it take us to recover? Will this critical decision require a complete process or system change? By asking these questions, we force ourselves as critical decision-makers to consider every possible outcome before deciding.

By looking at the lasting impact, we can uncover the decision's potential positive and negative consequences. Let's dig a little deeper here. To get a panoramic view of a critical decision, we must consider what we gain, lose, or must continue to endure because of the decision. Undoubtedly there will be positive residual benefits from the decision. This leads to too many erroneous decisions because only the positive was considered. Instant gratification often fails to consider the future. That's why it's called *instant.* The most effective decision-makers are willing to forego a splash decision that offers instant gratification in favor of a more difficult decision that provides a painful "right now" but delivers an ongoing benefit in the future.

Ironically, many delays in deciding are due to the instant pain derived from the decision. This process usually gives the *present* pain of the decision full attention while failing to consider the *residual* pain created by delaying the decision. Because the leader is unwilling to deal with the current pain of deciding, the leader puts himself or herself in a position to deal with ongoing pain. Therefore, considering residual costs and benefits is essential in the critical decision-making process.

The single most critical question a leader can ask himself or herself when considering the residual costs and benefits of a decision is "What happens in the future whether I make the decision or not?" When the leader takes the time to thoroughly vet this question by using some of the questions listed above, the leader can gain more confidence in his or her impending decision.

Let me remind you that many leaders do parts of this intuitively. Intuition is a very effective tool used by many leaders. However, intuition is only sometimes the best way to make decisions. One reason intuition may fail is a leader's misunderstanding of intuition—which is more than a gut feeling. Intuition is a perception of truth independent of any reasoning process. President Ronald Reagan famously quoted the Russian enjoinder "Trust but verify." You can trust your intuition if you verify. Verifying is the key to effectively quantifying the facts concerning your impending critical decision. Make sure you consider residual costs and benefits to your decision-making process, and you're sure to gain more confidence in your decisions.

The process should follow in this order:

a.   Honest evaluation (including self)

b.   Results—your list should be smaller at this point

c.   Transition to the last step

HONEST EVALUATION

There's another significant step in the quantification process: to accurately quantify the costs of a decision, you must include *honest evaluation* in this process, which is a willingness to assess yourself honestly as a decision-maker regarding your guiding principles, consistency, and emotions. It's simply human nature to make decisions based on your desire. I'm not suggesting that your desires don't matter. But the leader's desires must not outweigh good decision-making. The best decision-making relies on honesty and the best outcomes as determining factors in the final decision.

Only you know if your thought process concerning a critical decision is correctly aligned with your guiding principles. Remember that we talked earlier about your guiding principles and how to establish them and leverage them in the decision-making process. Your guiding principles were never intended to be established but not considered. They are designed to guide you on your leadership and decision-making journey. So as you honestly evaluate yourself in your decision-making process, consider having a printed copy of your guiding principles visible to help hold yourself accountable.

Consistency in your decision-making process creates credibility and demonstrates integrity. Every leader has an internal desire to be identified as a credible leader.

Credibility earns the team's confidence in their leader. When your team knows that you're a credible leader, they trust you. Trust is not quickly earned but can be easily forfeited. Credible leaders are given the benefit of the doubt because they are trusted leaders. But only the leader knows how credible he or she is. The leader must be honest in self-evaluation when it comes to credibility. Credibility is an area the leader cannot afford to neglect.

A credible leader is a leader with integrity. Leaders who have integrity do the right thing because it's the right thing to do. Integrity can simplify the decision-making process if the leader decides with integrity, which removes the gray areas from the decision-making process. That's a simple-enough concept. Well, maybe. Integrity eliminates wrong from decision-making, but only if the leader maintains his or her integrity when deciding. As a leader, you must continually evaluate your integrity honestly. Again, keep a printed copy of your guiding principles present to hold yourself accountable. Integrity is not optional for a leader. On a side note, integrity appears not only in your decision-making—it shows up in every area of your life. Commit to leading

> Trust is not quickly earned but can be easily forfeited.

and deciding with integrity in every area.

Guiding principles and integrity should have you covered when evaluating yourself honestly. Well, almost. Some other items like to bleed into the decision-making process, such as emotions. I tried to avoid this topic entirely in this book. After all, the title *is Critical Decisions Made Easy.* Of course, emotions are hardly easy. But at the risk of changing the desired outcome of this book, I'll touch on a few quick observations to help you with your emotions.

Your emotions are just that—*your* emotions. Often identified as *feelings,* they're present for many reasons. The easy way out is to allow yourself to respond to how you feel in any situation. Wouldn't that be easy? If someone frustrates you, you get angry. Someone does something you like, you get happy. If someone disrespects you, you fire the person. I think you can see where I'm going with this line of thinking.

The problem is that critical decision-making doesn't leave room for emotions as the basis of a decision. Leaders must be honest in their self-evaluation. Are you making this decision based on emotions? Whenever I coach executives, I encourage them to control their emotions before making any decision. A skilled leader can certainly pretend other actions do not emotionally influence him or her, but a leader of integrity knows when emotions are being considered in a decision.

Suppose the leader recognizes that he or she is being emotionally affected. In that case, the leader will press the pause button on the decision in order to reset, to gain control of his or her emotions, and proceed with the decision-making process. This takes great courage, but the leader willing to press the pause button will be viewed as a leader with integrity and credibility and can be trusted to make good decisions.

Take the time to evaluate yourself honestly. You'll enjoy the outcome!

RESULTS

Keep in mind that the goal of this process is to simplify the decision-making process. We have spent a bit of time on the quantification process. Remember: the first step in the process is *qualification.* So only some decisions will make it to the quantification process, as they could be eliminated as critical decisions in the qualification process. Each step in the process is designed to eliminate, disqualify, or move closer to a final decision for every decision a leader might face.

Now let's look back at the *quantification* process. We've learned that quantification determines the costs of the decision. As a decision-maker, I like getting to the desired outcome. As we develop processes and systems for our decision-making, much of the process becomes intuitive and second nature, but that happens only when we have consistent, proven processes that we are willing to implement.

Once we have qualified the decision as a critical decision that we must make and have counted the costs, we have what we need to decide confidently. The quantification process can take some time, but it's time well spent. It's essential to take advantage of this step. Take your time, go back, and ensure that you've thoroughly vetted each of the six steps in the quantification process:

1. Time

2. Money

3. Moral standards

4. Hard costs versus soft costs

5. The if-then process

6. Residual costs

Each step has a specific desired outcome. As you review each step, you'll gain more confidence in fully understanding the costs of the decision.

TRANSITION TO THE LAST STEP

As we prepare to move to the final step in the critical decision-making process, we want to ensure that we have thoroughly covered the qualification and quantification process. The leader's confidence must be strong enough to move forward without reservation. The real caution here is that many leaders make it to this point and stall. They get to the point at which they know exactly what to do, and for whatever reason, they get stuck. They become unwilling to make the decision. They put it to the side with no real urgency to get back to it.

Why do leaders get stuck at this point? What's stopping them from moving forward? In the next chapter we'll talk about how we get stuck, how to get unstuck, and how we get results, execute, or make the decision.

CHAPTER THREE

Execution

The final step in the critical decision-making process is execution. Dictionary.com defines *execution* as "to carry out, accomplish, do, or perform." While this is a self-explanatory and straightforward definition, execution is far from a simple process. Throughout this book our goal has been to develop systems and processes that build the decision-maker's confidence when making critical decisions. We all know that at some point we must make the decision—we must decide what we believe to be the best decision and be willing to live with the outcome.

Our attention to detail and building in some automation is all purposed to give us that much-needed confidence. In this final step of the decision-making process, I hope to help you overcome the various obstacles that prevent us from making the decision. We will consider four final steps in the process: Step 1: Mitigate Apprehension. Step 2: Be Decisive. Step 3: Activate Your Decision. Step 4: Be Accountable for Your Decision

STEP 1: MITIGATE APPREHENSION

When facing a critical decision, apprehension is understandably always present. When leaders face decisions they have deemed critical, a lot is riding on the decision. As a result, it's only natural to anticipate some adversity, misfortune, fear, or trouble. The natural mindset is usually focused on what can go wrong or the possible adverse outcomes of this decision.

Some may think it irresponsible if a leader fails to consider the possible adverse outcomes. I'm not suggesting that negative effects shouldn't be considered, but the potential adverse outcomes should not be the only considerations. There is the possibility of positive results as well.

A leader can be a super-optimistic decision-maker who expects every decision to end in the euphoria of success, bringing the delight of experiencing the desired outcome. Apprehension can display itself through either anxiety or excitement. Neither is fundamentally wrong, as both can serve as good indicators of the leader's position. Excitement and anxiety, however, are unreliable tools that cannot be counted on for consistency. If the leader leans toward anxiety, he or she risks never deciding. The anxious leader continually considers every possible flaw and failure of the decision. If not careful, he or she visualizes the catastrophic result of a decision and often replays the negative outcome from various viewpoints that keep him or her second-guessing every decision and even the capacity to make decisions.

Perhaps you have lived through this traumatizing nightmare yourself. You have fallen victim to the anxiety of decision-making. Again, this is not abnormal. Many leaders struggle with this process. This is not a bad thing. It's a good idea to take the critical decision-making process seriously. What you decide matters. The concern is legitimate, but the anxiety must be mitigated.

Excitement can have a very similar impact. The excited leader can often make critical decisions based on good feelings. I must admit that good feelings are great, but they're not a valid reason to decide. Yes, it's preferable to feel good about decisions, but sometimes that's not the case. Deciding to do what is best in no way guarantees feeling good.

Have you ever had to make the "right" decision that led you to a personal grief process? It was the right decision. The long-term outcome proved it was the right decision, but it didn't feel good at the time. That's why we can never let excitement or a good feeling be the stand-alone reason we make decisions. One of the key differences be-tween good leaders and great leaders is the ability to make the best decisions regardless of emotion or feelings. We're not to be emotionless when deciding, but we cannot rely on emotion alone, whether good or bad. Our excitement must be mitigated as well.

STEP 2: BE DECISIVE

The goal of every decision-maker is to be decisive. *Decisive* does not mean acting quickly; it simply means making good-quality, critical decisions efficiently. The transition from indecisive to decisive can seem like an infinite journey with many stressful stops.

Decisiveness produces confidence in the decision-maker and those impacted by the decision. When a leader can effectively and efficiently make decisions, the next decision is less threatening. Confidence begins to grow because it happened; the leader made the decision. When the leader feels confident in his or her decision, the team also gains confidence. Teams are more willing to follow a leader they can trust. Effective decision-making builds team confidence and leader trust. This place of decisiveness is not some unattainable, mythical destination. Decision-makers can make this muscle of decisiveness through developing processes and systems and via deliberate intentionality.

We spent the first portion of the book focusing on the qualification process. We learned that we must establish ground rules for making critical decisions, and we examined the three-step process of assessing, articulating, and aligning. The initial phase of making critical decisions, we learned, is to establish a process. When you develop a process or a system, the system helps you automate the decision-making process.

The power of systems is that once you build a reliable system that has been tested and adjusted as necessary, you have moved one step closer to being a decisive leader. The real key is to *trust* the process. We spend so much time developing systems because we can depend on them later. Many decision-makers have invested a great deal of time in devising systems, but they are unwilling to rely on the systems or even to implement them. This slows the process and prevents them from being decisive. The more intentional you are in developing your system on the front end, the more likely you are to depend on your system when faced with a critical decision.

Decisiveness doesn't just happen. As you build your systems and hold yourself accountable to using your systems, decisiveness becomes more natural. Some individuals are naturally wired as decisive people, but that's not the case for everyone. If you're naturally decisive, you must hold yourself accountable to develop systems that give you time to vet your decisiveness thoroughly. In other words, your system should include processes to ensure that you're not moving too quickly or for the wrong reasons. Decisiveness is desirable, but if not given the proper guardrails, it can get you in trouble.

Indecisiveness, on the other hand, can serve as an additional source of frustration for decision-makers. Process, in this case, provides the decision-maker with the confidence to make effective decisions more consistently. Many factors contribute to indecisiveness. Previous decision mishaps or failures are the most common offenders. Bad decisions have a way of constantly reminding you of your failure. You know how it goes—remember the last time you were in this position and you cost the company thousands of dollars? It was all your fault. Had you made a better decision, the company would have never been in that position. The failure keeps speaking to you as if it had a personal vendetta against you. I've learned that failures hold vendettas against you only when you empower them.

Failure occurs only when we don't learn the lesson in a particular situation. However, failure becomes our best lesson when we learn the lesson as we improve our decision-making. If you never make a bad or incorrect decision, you probably aren't making enough decisions. So ensure that you don't allow the last failure to impact your decisiveness negatively. Be willing to learn from failure. Be willing to improve your decision-making process—but *don't be afraid to make decisions.*

When looking to be decisive, the decision-maker must develop a process, deploy a process, and trust the process. Remember: accountability is critical. You must be willing to hold yourself accountable and even give other essential members of the team authority to hold you responsible for sticking with your processes. More consistent and effective decisions will be the day's outcome if you trust your process and become a decisive leader.

STEP 3: ACTIVATE YOUR DECISION

It seems hard to fathom that a decision-maker can get this far in the decision-making process but still not act on his or her decision. In reality, leaders often have a thoroughly vetted decision that has passed all the steps, meets every criterion, and causes him or her to feel confident. However, for whatever reason he or she will not activate the decision. This uncertainty causes the leader much unnecessary stress and exhaustion with this weight of undecided or yet-to-be-activated decisions.

The weight of stalled decisions creates many additional challenges for the decision-maker. First, as noted, there is unnecessary stress. Stress is something most leaders are far too familiar with. As an emotion, it impacts your ability to think or process information. It causes you to replay the decision to the point that stress can continually move from emotional distress to physical consequences. Stress can influence a leader's diet, exercise, or other physical activities and can cause him or her to become physically ill. A leader cannot afford to allow decisions to linger to the point that unmade decisions begin harming his or her emotional and physical health.

Delayed activation of the decision can also lead to slowed momentum in the business. When decisions begin stacking up, they add to what is an already overwhelming workload. Just think about it. You have one or two decisions you need to activate, but again, you don't do it for whatever reason. The one or two decisions soon become three or four, and before you know it, your stress is at an all-time high while your business is slowing to an all-time low. This happens not because you have not made the decisions but because you failed to activate them.

Quite frankly, I could go on and on about the negative consequences of getting right to the point of decision activation but failing to activate. As leaders we face many challenges daily. The more significant challenge is in finding solutions. We all know we must execute the decision, but we get stuck on the *how.*

How do we execute this next step in the decision-making process? It's simple, right? "Just do it," to borrow a slogan from Nike—right? Or maybe we could use the philosophy of 1970s comic book and television show characters "the Wonder Twins." They would say, "Wonder Twin powers, activate the shape of . . ." and they would state whatever they needed to become at that moment, and it would happen. What if we said, "Decision-making powers, activate!" in the shape of an accurate decision? If it were only that simple! At some point the leader must activate his or her decisions. To get through this process phase, the leader must be comfortable, confident, and courageous.

Comfort can be so subjective. To be comfortable with a decision means to be at ease with it. That sounds simple enough. Well, not exactly. Comfort is subject to what brings an individual relief. What does it take to make you comfortable with a decision? Does it mean to remove all anxiety? Does it mean not upsetting anyone when you deliver the decision? What may bring comfort to one leader may not bring comfort to another. So we must figure this comfort thing out because we know it will help us to activate our decision. Since comfort is subjective, we must take a personal inventory of what makes us comfortable with a decision. It's unreasonable to think that we'll ever get completely

> At some point the leader must activate his or her decisions.

comfortable with all decisions. Sure, there will be some decisions we're entirely comfortable with. Still, we must develop another system to help us to be as comfortable as possible with our decisions.

Remember: we're talking about critical decisions. While in pursuit of comfort, we must have a way to get "comfortable" even if we're not 100-percent comfortable. We must rely on the system that brought us to this point in the first place. Remember: we have gone through the qualification and quantification processes already. We know how the decision meets our various standards because we have worked the system. We have taken the time and been very intentional in our process to run the decision through the wringer. If the decision has survived to this point, the leader must be willing to trust the system to provide the necessary level of comfort required to activate the decision. Comfort in its most desired form may not be possible when making critical decisions, but leaders can be comfortable with their process. Invest the time on the front end to build a strong system, and trust the system to bring you enough comfort to activate the decision.

Although comfort means feeling good about the decision, confidence is slightly different, taking comfort to the next level. Confidence says, "I know this is the right decision." When a decision-maker lacks confidence in each decision, he or she often delays the decision activation. Why?

Because confidence comes with consequences. Confidence is necessary because it carries weight beyond just the decision itself. The team's confidence in their leader either increases or decreases based on the success or failure of decisions. People believe in you and trust you when you make good decisions. When you make poor decisions, the team may question your leadership. Beyond that, leaders want to get it right. Leaders want to make the right decision every time. Of course, there's no way a leader can get it right every time. Some decisions will be wrong with all the systems, instincts, gut feelings, or even the flip of a coin.

> A leader must be confident in his or her processes and systems.

So how does a leader gain confidence in decisions? A leader must be confident in his or her processes and systems. A leader must ask, "Have I done my homework? Have I been objective in my assessment according to my pre-established criterion concerning the critical decision? Have I focused on facts, not emotions?" By asking these questions, a leader can be confident in making the best decision. Confidence in a decision is not contingent on whether the decision is right or wrong but on answering the question "Is this the best decision for this situation?" So confidence is based on the process, not necessarily the outcome.

With that in mind, processes must be evaluated regularly and modified as necessary. The critical point is that yesterday's model may not work in today's environment. If you want to have confidence in your processes and systems, you must spend the time to make sure that your processes and systems are still relevant and that you're using the best tools for the best possible outcomes.

Finally, it takes courage to activate the decision. Courage is the quality of mind or spirit that enables a person to face difficulty, danger, pain, and so on without fear. So now we get to the heart of the matter. Demonstrating courage in the face of a critical decision is easier said than done. Just by being identified as a leader, we know that courage is a characteristic that must be present. Often implied, not stated, it is expected that leaders have a tremendous amount of courage, and it comes naturally. Although that's probably a true statement on some levels, the truth is that most leaders battle internally with courage more than they're willing to share or display externally. Leaders like to present as cool, calm, and collected, but many times there are numerous internal fears they struggle to keep hidden as they try mustering up the inner fortitude to put on a courageous front.

As a result, they put more pressure on themselves than required to make a critical decision.

So how does a leader transition from attempting to present courage to possessing courage and demonstrating this courage in a critical decision-making process? I know—this is a million-dollar question. Courage does not magically appear. Courage is built over time through experience. Just consider that experienced leaders struggle less with courage than inexperienced leaders. That's not to say that experienced leaders don't struggle with courage, but I believe it's fair to say they may struggle less than inexperienced leaders. But why? Because the journey of getting experience creates the comfort and the confidence that contribute to a leader's courage. Experience is valuable because it teaches you decision-making dos and don'ts.

> Courage is built over time through experience.

Experience leverages the lessons that would otherwise be called failure to instruct the leader on the *how* and the *why* in the decision-making process.

On the front end of developing the decision-making process, there needs to be a road map. As you make more and more decisions, the better you understand the whole process of decision-making. There are the pre-decision, decision, and post-decision components of the decision-making process. We've spent much time in this book talking about the pre-decision element. We've taken an in-depth look at the qualification and quantification processes. A little bit later we will talk more about the post-decision part of the process. But for now I want to highlight how what you learn after the decision can help you have the courage required to make the next decision. When you're willing to learn from an intentional panoramic perspective, courage becomes more accessible because you're prepared to make the decision and understand the consequences.

So now you're comfortable with the decision. You're confident in the decision. You have the courage to execute the decision. So—*execute* the decision!

STEP 4: BE ACCOUNTABLE FOR YOUR DECISION

Now that you've finally activated the decision, what's next? The hard part is over. The most challenging part of the journey is the painstaking part of the process to the point at which you can activate the decision. You did it! It may be too soon to know the accuracy or outcome of the decision, but it's off your desk! So take a moment to refresh yourself. That means refusing the immediate temptation to move on to the next pressing matter in your inbox. There will be time for that later, but give yourself a mental break now. Remember: the critical decision-making model is reserved for only the most critical decisions. You'll have more than your fair share of decisions to qualify for this status, but it should be a short list. You've built systems and processes to ensure that you're not overwhelmed with unqualified "critical" decisions.

Okay, your break is over. Back to our original question: You have activated the decision—now what? Now it's time to watch the decision go from activation to maturation. Now you get to see the outcomes of the decision. *Did it work? Was it the right decision? Did I get the results I thought I would get? Who was impacted? How did the affected parties receive it?* The list of questions could go on and on. The critical thing to remember as a decision-maker is that you are responsible for all the questions above and also those not listed. Let me restate that *you* are responsible for *all* the questions above.

As the decision-maker, you are accountable or answerable for all outcomes of your decision. Did you notice I said *your* decision? I'm sure you've heard the old phrase made famous by the thirty-third president of the United States, Harry S. Truman, "The buck stops here." President Truman reportedly kept a sign with that phrase on his desk in the Oval Office with the inference that the president must make the decisions *and* accept the ultimate responsibility for whatever decisions are made. Now, I'm not suggesting you make presidential-level decisions with global implications, but you're making decisions that will impact your world, and the proverbial buck stops with you.

So how do you really hold yourself accountable beyond just taking responsibility for your decisions? The critical component of holding yourself accountable is ensuring that you never "pass the buck." The easy thing to do in a difficult decision is to blame someone else for a less-than-desirable outcome. Many factors are considered when coming to a final decision. Often there is information that may not have been presented or even available at the time of the decision. It's even possible that someone on your team failed to share critical information that may have impacted your decision. These are genuine possibilities, but possibilities should never be used as excuses to blame someone else for *your* decision.

Since it's your decision, you must take full responsibility for every aspect of it, the known and the unknown. Your processes and systems are intended to ensure that you have as much information as possible regarding every decision. There will be some instances in which you cannot get all the information you would like, but the decision and the outcome still belong to you. Your team may not like your decision, but they will respect you more if you accept responsibility.

When you refuse to "pass the buck," you make it clear that you own your decisions. To own a decision means owning the outcome, whether good or bad. Owning your decisions is an excellent way to demonstrate your integrity and character. Being willing to own your decisions can help structure how others present information to you.

When my daughters were growing up, they would of course often come to me with requests. I had a very well-known requirement: "If you have a request, you must have a plan." My daughters learned this concept and understood it well. As a result, when they would come to me, they didn't just make a simple request—they also had a plan. My older daughter, Danielle, the more social one, would come well prepared for the battery of questions she knew I would have based on her previous requests. The conversation would usually go something like this:

> When you refuse to "pass the buck," you make it clear that you own your decisions.

Danielle: "Daddy, can I go to Chelsea's house for a party next Friday?"

Me: "What's the occasion? Who will be there? Will her parents be there? Will there be any boys there?" (You know, just the basic information a daddy needs to know)

Danielle: "It's for her birthday, and her mom and dad will be there, along with other parents. Yes, there will be boys there, but they're all from my class, and you've met them. You remember Chad, don't you?"

As you can tell by the dialogue, Danielle was ready to answer the questions she knew I would have. Why? Because in previous situations we had already gone through this process. She learned the requirements for me to decide, so she positioned the request in the best way for me to say yes. When you own your decisions, those around you know what to expect and are more likely to respect you. Own your decisions.

I have one more consideration I would like to share regarding holding yourself accountable for your decisions. Be sure that as you own the decision, you spend time reviewing the outcomes of your decision. Reviewing your decision is to reveal the good, the bad, and the ugly. You want to look at the positive results, the adverse outcomes, and even the regrettable outcomes. This process is not to facilitate a celebration for your good outcomes or chastise yourself for your adverse outcomes or get depressed over your unfortunate outcomes. The purpose of the review is to learn. Learn what you did right, what you could do better, and what you should never do again.

Getting this information is the first step in your next decision. Well, not so fast. This information can be the first

> Accountability requires a commitment to learn and grow from what you know.

step in your next critical decision, but only if you're willing to modify your existing processes and systems accordingly. Accountability requires a commitment to learn and grow from what you know. In essence, we have to activate our accountability. Make sure you do not review the decision to validate your good decisions and reveal the flaws of your poor decisions; use your review as an opportunity to *revise your processes*. Adding this to your process will give you more comfort, confidence, and courage to make effective critical decisions!

EXECUTION WRAP-UP

Execution anchors the "Critical Decisions Made Easy" process. Let's take a quick look back at the execution process:

Step 1 – Mitigate Apprehension

Step 2 – Be Decisive

Step 3 – Activate Your Decision

Step 4 – Be Accountable for Your Decision

In Step 1, "Mitigate Apprehension," we learned to look at anxiety as a positive and to consider all possible outcomes, not just the negative. This is key in the critical decision-making process. A leader's mindset can completely redirect his or her decision-making experience. The apprehension must never be overlooked or discredited. Apprehension or anxiety is real, and a leader often does not take the time to understand himself or herself. How various components of the decision-making process impact the leader can add unnecessary stress to his or her life. Remember that as a decision-making leader, you should anticipate adversity. Do not be surprised by the inevitable. When you expect that you'll experience some adversity, you can plan for it! You can build barriers to help protect you during those times. Barriers do not prevent adversity—they help protect you from it and give you the means to deal with it.

In Step 2 we learned to "Be Decisive." Decisiveness requires leaders to build systems they trust to put themselves in the best possible position. We learned that decisiveness helps a leader develop confidence in his or her decision-making and helps the team to believe in the leader. Remember: an under-informed leader will find it very difficult to be decisive. Information, facts, and data are a decisive leader's friend. Some leaders have excellent instincts or strong gut feelings. I have good instincts and a pretty good "gut." Still, I would encourage you to remember to "trust but verify." It's okay to trust your gut instincts if you verify. Your decisions are too critical to make without facts and data. When you have the information, it's then easier to make the correct decision. Be decisive! *Trust but verify!*

In Step 3 we learned what proves to be the most challenging part of the execution process: "Activate Your Decision." Activation is best facilitated by looking backward. When you take the time to look back at your process and systems, you gain confidence that you're making the best decision for this situation. Keep in mind that the best decision may be right only sometimes. The best decision based on the circumstances may differ from the decision you desire to make. Remember that you have systems and processes to help you stay within your guidelines.

Critical decisions are complex, and it stands to reason that we'll only sometimes get them right. I know that's challenging, but who do you know who gets every decision right? No one, of course! But just because no one gets every decision right, that does not justify not giving your best. Activate your decisions with comfortability, confidence, and courage, knowing you have thor-

> It's okay to trust your gut instincts if you verify.

oughly arrived at a decision. Now, "decision-making powers, activate!"

In Step 4 we learned that you must be accountable or answerable for your decisions. As a decision-maker, the buck stops with you. When considering accountability, you learned to own your decisions and refuse to "pass the buck." Owning your decisions means owning the outcomes of your decisions, whether good or bad. Remember that it's important to ask yourself a few questions: *Did it work? Was it the right decision? Did I get the results I thought I would get? Who was impacted? How did the affected parties receive it?* The critical thing to remember as a decision-maker is that you are responsible for all the questions above and those not listed. Let me restate that *you* are responsible for *all* the questions above. Being responsible for your decisions allows you to create a process with your team that will build integrity with your team and equip you with information to help you make better decisions.

Take the time to review the outcomes of your decisions. Be willing to modify your processes when the evidence reveals opportunity for growth. As you continue sharpening your decision-making process, you continue improving your comfort and confidence in your decision-making process. Be accountable for your decisions!

We have covered a lot of information in the execution phase of the critical decision-making process. Still, once you add structure to your decision-making, you'll find it much easier to make an effective decision. So let's keep in mind the four steps to execution: (1) Mitigate Apprehension, (2) Be Decisive, (3) Activate Your Decision, (4) Be Accountable for Your Decision.

So what should you take away from this? You need to *build a* process for your critical decision-making. By now you have intentionally built a process. It may not be perfect, but it's a very good start. Now that you've built your process, you need to *remember* your process. Far too many great ideas, strategies, and plans stay on the board room whiteboard or in the "good ideas" file. Your new decision-making process will not be the next great idea that does not get off the ground. Get your process off the paper and out of the clouds—and use it! Better yet, don't just use your process—*reuse* your process. As you reuse your process, you'll *refine* your process. This is just the beginning! Excellent decision-making is in your view!

QUALIFY – QUANTIFY – EXECUTE! Critical decisions made easy!

CONCLUSION

What a fantastic journey! You have taken a journey to develop and deploy your critical decision-making process. Let's pick back up where we started. Remember the story I opened the book up with in the introduction, the one about the kid who had a job that he thought was a career until life showed him otherwise? Whatever happened to that kid?

Well, in December 1996 I received that associate degree in applied science (finance) after five grueling years of part-time school, full-time employment, full-time marriage, full-time parenting, part-time ministry, and a few other odd jobs here and there. Wow—I got tired just typing that! I ended up staying with that company for over twenty years. Despite a few mergers and acquisitions along the way, I stayed with the business. Over the years I continued getting many promotions and experienced tremendous growth throughout my career.

Now let's go back to the first critical decision. The decision was to take advantage of the tuition reimbursement program and return to college for the third or fourth time. Although the decision seemed like a no-brainer, it really wasn't. At the time my schedule was over-packed, and my need for money was immediate.

I had to go through the process of *qualifying*. Should I go to school or not? The answer is that I needed to, but it was more complicated than that. Based on my guiding principles, the stage of life I was in, and my family considerations, this decision qualified as critical. I believed in doing things the right way. As a person of faith, I took the role and responsibility of the head of the house very seriously. I believed my responsibility was to care for and provide for my family. I have an amazing wife who has supported me for over thirty-two years. Even during this stage of life, she was willing to get a part-time job while pregnant with our oldest daughter to help our financial ends to meet. But I still felt the pressure and the burden to take care of my family! I was taught from an early age to work hard and that everything else would then take care of itself. And again, it was my job to take care of the family. At the time this was a critical decision.

Then I had to move on to the *quantification* process. It was time to count the costs. This seems intuitive, but when you're facing bankruptcy and feel overwhelmed by your responsibilities, there's little time to count costs. There were so many considerations. Do I have time to go to school? If I go, will it make a difference in my financial situation? Can I get where I want to be financially if I choose *not* to go to school? Can my wife handle my being gone another night? How long is five years? It seemed like an eternity. What about my other part-time jobs (side hustles)? Can I still do them? I anticipate that we'll need money in the future, but we need cash now!

These were just a few of the considerations in my quantification process, and I mean a few. I had to seriously consider all these things. But wait—there's more. Where do I want to be five or ten years from now? Remember that this was the early 1990s, so not everything was moving at the speed of light yet. Back in those days we did ten-year or even twenty-year plans. I know my Generation Z readers are asking, "Who does that? *Twenty*-year plans?" But it was a thing back in the good ol' days.

Once I struggled through the quantification process, it was on to *execution*! You want to talk about apprehension or anxiety? I must have felt every emotion possible to humanity when I decided to return to college. The evidence was clear—I had no choice. I had to invest in my future. My family depended on it. My career depended on it. My self-worth depended on it. Even though I knew I could do it (meaning handle going to school and doing the work), I struggled with committing to activating my decision. I was not decisive or willing to trust the process at all. The truth is that I did not have a process. Some thirty-plus years later, I can try to unscramble what happened. But at that point in my life and career, I was flying by the seat of my pants at best.

In the execution phase of the critical decision-making process, I encourage you to build your strategy, remember your process, and reuse your process. Going back through my first critical decision, I can now determine two things. Number one, the process worked. I received the best possible outcome from the decision to go back to school. Number two, even without a codified process, I began using this model. So the result of the decision to go back to school, made in my early 20s, became the process I've shared with you in this book.

The exciting thing about this process is that it works in every area of your life. I've applied these same three steps of qualification, quantification, and execution in multiple areas of my life, and they work. Whether the decision was academic, professional, spiritual, health and wellness-related, or family-and-friends-related, it has consistently worked.

I have even used this system when working with others to help them through their critical decision-making processes. There are a few underlying requirements to make this system work for you. I will take the last paragraphs to give you those requirements. Effective decision-making requires competence, consistency, and commitment.

The entire journey of this book is about developing systems and processes to be utilized in effective critical decision-making resulting in desired outcomes. One of the underlying qualifiers for effective decision-making is competence. *Competence,* according to Dictionary.com, is "the possession of required skill, knowledge, or qualification." The decision-maker must be competent to make the best possible decision and achieve the best possible outcome. Competence can be developed in various ways. My focus here is not on the specific *how* of competence but on the willingness to dedicate yourself to achieving the competence needed at your decision-making level. In brief, competence is gained through education, formal or otherwise, and experience.

When I say *education,* however, I'm not restricting education to a formal learning process through a traditional institution of higher education. I'm a proponent of higher education, declaring a major, and obtaining your degree. Pursuing advanced degrees is an acceptable way of developing your competence. You can also gain education through the old tried-and-true on-the-job training method. You can learn by watching and doing on the job. These are both effective ways to get an education.

Additionally, you could get a business or life coach to train you. Vocational and technical education schools are also options. What is most important is to make sure that your last educational achievement is not your final academic achievement. Education is an ongoing process that ensures that you're competent to make whatever decision you face.

One final thought on competence. You may face some decisions that fall outside of your area of competence. What do you do then? You take the advice of American game show host Regis Philbin of *Who Wants to Be a Millionaire?* and use a lifeline. Regis gave the contestant four choices: phone a friend, fifty-fifty, poll the audience, or ask one person from the audience. If you lack competence, I suggest researching and "phoning a friend" who is competent to help you make the decision. Not all decisions are created equal, so use your resources. When you *operate* with competence, you can *work* with confidence.

Competence is best supported by consistency. Consistency can be a big challenge for leaders and decision-makers alike. Consistency means always adhering to the same principles, course, or form. Earlier in the book we worked to establish guiding principles, which must be something other than part-time principles. You took the time to develop your guiding principles to remove inconsistencies from the decision-making process. Remember: guiding principles are based on your personal beliefs and values. Your belief system and personal beliefs establish the boundaries and guidelines for how you lead every area of your life. The decision-making process becomes more consistent when guiding principles are in place *and* adhered to. We all need these guidelines to help us stay on the path we desire to be on.

A couple of factors always seem to be in opposition to consistency: time and fatigue. Leaders' schedules are often over-filled with life; as a result, we sometimes feel pressured to take shortcuts to save time. It's saving time only if we don't have to pay the time back later. An inconsistent, rushed decision-making process is sure to come with consequences. Rushing on the front end of a decision almost always comes with having to revisit the same decision, which takes more time.

> The decision-making process becomes more consistent when guiding principles are in place *and* adhered to.

How do you avoid this trap? Make up your mind that you'll follow your systems all the time. Many decision-makers adopt processes they don't believe in, which can result in dissatisfied decision-makers. Remember: this is your process. You created the process from start to finish. You have taken the time to review and revise your process. Why would you expose yourself to unintended consequences you built a system to avoid? Make up your mind always to be active in your process so you can be a satisfied decision-maker!

The other consideration is commitment. Are you committed to your processes? It's your process. You've established it, but are you willing to commit? Indeed, this is easier said than done. I know it sounded good when you said you would do it, but you're now questioning the idea for many different reasons. You find yourself talking yourself into some decisions while simultaneously talking yourself out of other decisions. The key

> Decision-making stands at the center of your success.

to commitment is discipline, which is developed through learning. We have already covered the educational component of competence. Education is where you learn the disciplines you desire to adhere to, and commitment is where discipline shows up.

Commitment is a mindset. Commitment is your choice. You get to decide how you'll obligate your time and talents. Commitment is a willful choice to do or not to do. Effective decision-making is only one tool in a successful leader's tool bag. It's an essential tool, but a tool nonetheless. Decision-making stands at the center of your success. Leaders who make good decisions are usually successful. In turn, successful leaders are committed leaders. Just think about the most successful leaders you know. They wake up early and often read many books, magazines, and periodicals. They may not have these specific disciplines, but rest assured—they have disciplines they're committed to. I call them their "guiding principles."

One of the most inspiring books I have read is *You Owe You,* by Dr. Eric Thomas. He calls things that you're committed to your "non-negotiables." It would be best if you committed to your guiding principles to succeed along your leadership journey. Your guiding principles apply to every area of your life every day.

THANK YOU

Thank you for reading *Critical Decisions Made Easy.* This book is truly a passion project for me. I had no idea that a decision in my twenties would become a resource to so many. Along this journey I have made my share of good decisions as well as not-so-good ones. But with each decision came a lesson. I have had to "retake" some decision lessons along the way, but each decision prepared me for the next decision.

Thank you for believing in yourself as a leader and being open to exploring *Critical Decisions Made Easy* as a potential resource to help you in your decision-making process. I'm sure you are already doing many things in this book, at least in part. You have more experience and education than you might give yourself credit for. But I hope this book has helped you bring it all together for the next step on your journey to success.

I want to challenge you. What decision have you put off far too long? Perhaps you've made the decision but still need to activate it. Is it a book you are supposed to write? Maybe a screenplay. Do you have a passion you've muted so long that you've decided it could never happen? I have a question: *Why can't it happen?* What excuses are you giving voice to? What—are you too old? Has your time already passed? Is it that you don't have the money? My friend, these are all excuses.

Let me pause here and share a quick story with you in hopes of helping you make the critical decision to do it now! In 2017 I had the opportunity to publish my first book, *90 Days of Believing God.* Exciting, right? Well, you may not think so after I tell you this story. The book idea started in 2009. Yes, you read it correctly—published in 2017 but begun in 2009. I had a complete outline with all my supporting content in 2009 and started to write a little and tell people I was writing a book.

From 2009 to early 2017 I was committed to writing my first book! I was so "committed" that I wrote fewer than 1,000 words per year for the first six years! So—you can see that I really wasn't committed at all. Maybe I was committed to an idea, but I could not be found guilty of committing to the project. I made every excuse in the book. I started at the place of "I can't write a book" and then moved on to "I don't have a publisher, I don't have any money, I can't sell a book, I'm too busy to write a book"—and the list goes on and on.

The problem wasn't what I was claiming in any of those excuses. The problem was that I had not decided to finish writing a book! In 2017, sensing my frustration with writing the book and the process, my older daughter asked me, "Daddy, have you given yourself a deadline to finish the book? You never miss your deadlines." So there you have it. The same daughter I taught systems to early in her childhood reminded me of the systems I already had in place. She reminded me that I typically set a deadline when something was important to me. When I make a decision, it's essential; whatever it is gets a deadline, a strategy, measurements, and accountability. *But it all starts with the decision.*

Because of the decision to write my first book, you're now reading my *third* book! I'll begin my fourth book as soon as I finish the last few paragraphs of this one. Your effective critical decisions help you make the next critical decision. I learned the lesson of the process by being reminded by my daughter of a process I once used but failed to transfer. It wasn't a new lesson, just a forgotten lesson. Remember that in the execution phase I challenged you to remember your process. This book is a product of remembering.

I share this story with you hoping it will motivate you to activate the decision you made years ago but that you're still trying to talk yourself out of. You didn't decide by accident or for no reason—you decided because something inside you said you needed to do this. Well, I agree with the something in you that said you need to do this, and I believe you can do it! *Activate your decision today!* Don't delay for another second. Put the decision back on the consideration table and qualify, quantify, and execute—today!

I'm committed to living my life in a way that consistently adds value to others. From the bottom of my heart, thank you for allowing me to add value to you. I want you to know that I care about you, and I care about your success. Your decision to activate your decision will add value to someone else's life. And there's a bonus to having the opportunity to add value to someone else's life. When you add value to someone else's life, you get the fulfillment of having had the opportunity to make a difference in that person's life.

Finally, every critical decision you make impacts more people than you may ever know. The decision to have that crucial conversation with that difficult employee could easily lead to a rehabilitated employee changing his or her entire life approach—all because you took the time to have the critical conversation instead of terminating him or her. Now the person's family receives the residual benefits of your critical decision.

Thank you again for the opportunity to add value to you. Until next time, let's keep growing together!

How to Use the Critical Decision-Making Assessment—Business (CDMA—B) Tool

Here you will find ten considerations you can apply when making your business decisions. Questions are provided, each of which gives a brief description to help you formulate your criteria and rate each consideration effectively. The rating for each consideration is 0 – 10, with 0 being the lowest and 10 being the highest, concerning the consideration being the best fit for you. Note: when using the CDMA—B tool, you are not comparing one decision to another but rather rating each component of the individual decision to create a composite score, which determines how well the decision works for you as a stand-alone decision.

For example, question one is "How does this decision align with my guiding principles?" Earlier in the book we went through the process of establishing guiding principles. You will recall that guiding principles can qualify or disqualify a decision (research). When using the CDMA—B tool, you will consider the decision as it relates to your guiding principles. For instance, if one of your guiding principles is never to do anything that negatively impacts the environment, but the current decision hurts the environment, you would score it very low. On the other hand, if the decision is a pro-environment decision, you would give it a higher score.

Remember: the CDMA—B tool is not a comparison tool between possible decisions. Rather, its purpose is to help you determine how well the decision aligns with you as an individual. Some decisions work well for you but may not work well for others. Your goal is to put yourself in the best possible position to achieve the best possible outcome by making the best possible decision.

Three considerations are given for each question, designed to help challenge your thought process when making decisions. Remember that you're building a decision-making system that positions you always to make the best possible decision. Now work through the sample CDMA—B assessment tool and try it on your next decision. If you want to do this electronically, please visit *rodneyrpayne.com* to use the free assessment tool.

1. How does this decision align with my guiding principles?
   - Identify your guiding principles
     (they should be static)
   - Honor your guiding principles
   - Demonstrate your guiding principles

2. How well does this decision align with my core competencies?
   - Am I qualified for the opportunity?
   - Can I acquire the skills?
   - Is it challenging enough to keep my attention?

3. How much fulfillment does this decision provide for me?
   - Does the opportunity give me joy?
   - Am I passionate about it?
   - Can I grow while doing it?

4. How well does this decision help meet my financial goals?
   - Does it meet my financial needs?
   - Are the financial provisions sustainable?
   - Is there a limiting cap?

5. How well does this decision align with my personal/business goals?
   - Does the opportunity align with my personal/business goals?

- Does the opportunity align with my short-term, mid-range, and long-term goals?
- Am I settling for this opportunity?

6. How well does this decision align with my personal/business purpose?
   - Does the opportunity align with my *why?*
   - Does the opportunity require me to sacrifice my real purpose?
   - Does the opportunity allow me to grow in my purpose?

7. How compatible am I with the leadership regarding this decision?
   - Do I believe in the leadership of the organization?
   - Am I a good fit for the leadership style of the organization?
   - Can I add value to the organization's leadership?

8. How well do I fit with the brand/company/people?
   - Do I believe in the brand?
   - Am I a good fit for the brand?
   - Does the brand have a good reputation?

9. How well do I match the culture of the organization?
    *   How does the brand function?
    *   How does the brand operate behind the scenes?
    *   Does the culture align with my guiding principles?

10. How well does the decision meet my security needs?
    *   Is the brand stable?
    *   Is the product relevant and sustainable?
    *   Can I grow safely to my next level?

CRITICAL DECISION-MAKING ASSESSMENT-BUSINESS TOOL

1. How does this decision align with my guiding principles?

1	2	3	4	5	6	7	8	9	10

Not well   Somewhat   Very well

2. How well does this decision align with my core competencies?

1	2	3	4	5	6	7	8	9	10

Not well   Somewhat   Very well

3.　How well does this decision provide fulfillment for me?

| 1 | 2 | 3 | 4 | 5 | 6 | 7 | 8 | 9 | 10 |

Not well　　　　　　　　Somewhat　　　　　　Very well

4.　How well does this decision help meet my financial goals?

| 1 | 2 | 3 | 4 | 5 | 6 | 7 | 8 | 9 | 10 |

Not well　　　　　　　　Somewhat　　　　　　Very well

5.　How well does this decision align with my personal/business goals?

| 1 | 2 | 3 | 4 | 5 | 6 | 7 | 8 | 9 | 10 |

Not well　　　　　　　　Somewhat　　　　　　Very well

6.　How well does this decision align with my personal/business purpose?

| 1 | 2 | 3 | 4 | 5 | 6 | 7 | 8 | 9 | 10 |

Not well　　　　　　　　Somewhat　　　　　　Very well

7. How well am I being compatible with the leadership regarding this decision?

| 1 | 2 | 3 | 4 | 5 | 6 | 7 | 8 | 9 | 10 |

Not well   Somewhat   Very well

8. How well do I fit with the brand/company/people?

| 1 | 2 | 3 | 4 | 5 | 6 | 7 | 8 | 9 | 10 |

Not well   Somewhat   Very well

9. How well do I match the culture of the organization?

| 1 | 2 | 3 | 4 | 5 | 6 | 7 | 8 | 9 | 10 |

Not well   Somewhat   Very well

10. How well does the decision meet my security needs?

| 1 | 2 | 3 | 4 | 5 | 6 | 7 | 8 | 9 | 10 |

Not well   Somewhat   Very well

TOTAL SCORE: _____

≤ 65   =   **Poor.** This decision is unlikely to work out for you.

66—80 =   **Possible.** This decision could work but is not likely a good long-term decision.

81—90 =   **Better.** This decision has an opportunity to work. Be careful not to compromise in critical areas.

90—100 =   **Best.** This decision has the best opportunity to work. Pay close attention to your guiding principles and security in vetting the decision.

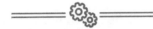

ABOUT THE AUTHOR

Rodney R. Payne is a goal-driven family man who understands the power of decision-making and taking action firsthand. He has over twenty-five years of experience rebuilding teams and excels at helping leaders and their teams get to the next level without giving them a cookie-cutter approach. His customized, proven techniques have increased the bottom line of both small businesses and Fortune 500 companies worldwide through his company "One Voice Leadership." Rodney is a Maxwell Leadership Certified Team Executive Program Leader. He is the host of the leadership podcast "Speaking with One Voice," an author, coach, speaker, and trainer whose energetic and witty approach captivates and ignites the fire inside of people, helping them grow to the next level in their leadership journey. He will *engage, energize,* and *equip* you with all the tools you need to navigate life and the workplace while becoming your best self.